HOW TO USE THIS BOOK

This Wild Wonder Workbook is designed to help children explore the natural world through creativity and curiosity.

Inside this book, children will:

- Observe animals and their environments

- Practice drawing, tracing, and problem-solving

- Learn facts about wildlife and habitats

- Use their imagination to build their own scenes and stories

Each page invites young explorers to slow down, look closely, and think about how animals live in the world around them. There are no wrong answers. Children are encouraged to color, draw, imagine, and create freely.

LEARNING BEGINS WITH CURIOSITY!

Angelfish

Fish

Angelfish glide through coral reefs like jewels of the sea. Their long fins flutter as they slip between rocks and seaweed, always looking for places to hide. In the reef, they stay safe among bright coral and other small fish. Can you draw coral and sea plants around this angelfish to make the reef complete?

Octopus

Octopus

SQUEEZE ME!

Octopuses can fit into the strangest places. Even tiny cups! One is already tucked inside the glass here. Now it's your turn!

Can you draw another octopus squeezing into the empty cup beside it?

Octopuses are clever creatures of the sea. They can squeeze into the smallest spaces, hiding in coral crevices, seashells, and even empty bottles on the ocean floor. With eight twisty arms and quick thinking, an octopus always finds a way to stay safe and sneaky. Can you imagine where one might try to hide next?

Crab

Crab

SECURITY GUARD

Crabs share the reef with many creatures! This one lives near coral and seaweed, but who else might move in?

Can you draw a few sea animals swimming nearby to keep the crab company?

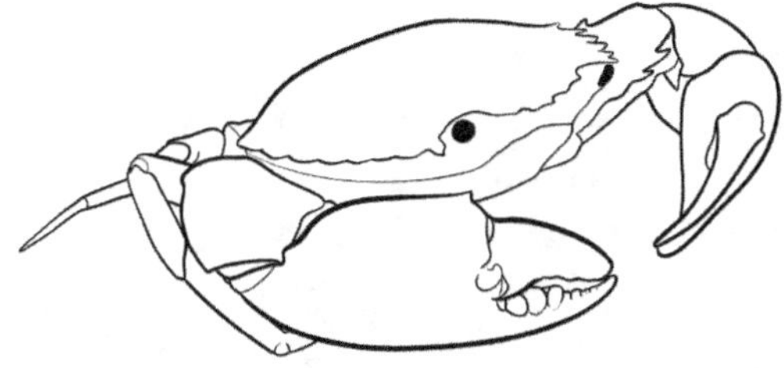

Crabs scuttle sideways across the sandy ocean floor, moving quickly between coral and seaweed. Their tough shells protect them from bigger animals, and sometimes they even carry shells or seaweed as decorations. Can you draw more coral, seaweed, and shells around this crab to help it feel safe in its reef home?

Dolphin

Dolphin

———

Dolphins leap and play in the waves, swimming together in groups called pods. They use squeaks and clicks to talk to each other as they chase fish and ride the rolling surf. Can you draw splashing waves and other dolphins nearby so this one isn't swimming alone?

Whale

Whale

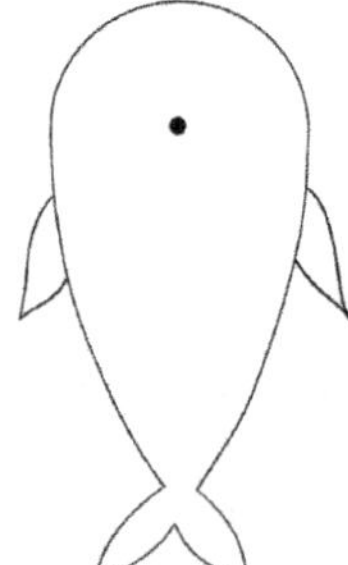

WANDERLUST

Whales typically travel long distances across the ocean.

Can you draw a make-believe island that this whale may want to swim to, and then draw a line from the whale to show which island it chooses?

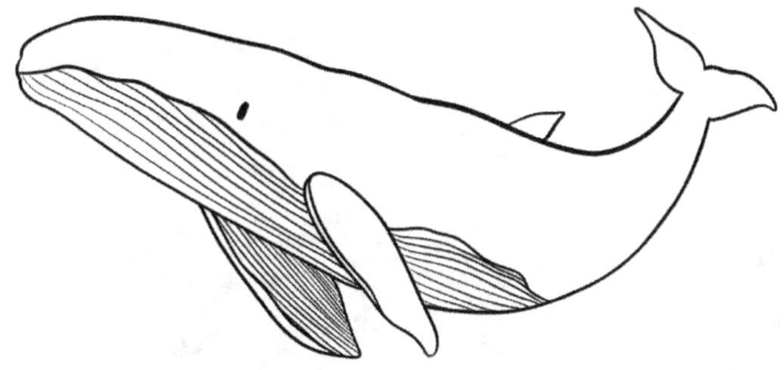

Blue whales are the largest animals on Earth. They glide through the open ocean, diving deep to find tiny shrimp-like creatures called krill. Even though they are enormous, blue whales move with gentle grace, traveling thousands of miles across the seas. Can you draw this giant in the deep ocean?

Clownfish

Clownfish

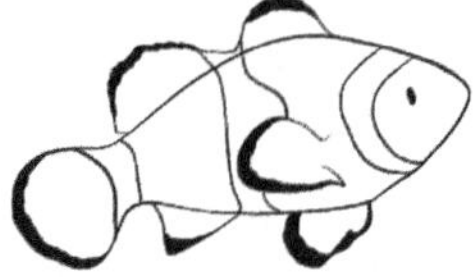

SECRET HIDEAWAY

Clownfish love to hide in safe places like coral, seaweed, or anemones. Two of these clownfish already have hiding spots, but one is still out in the open! Can you draw a special hiding place for the last clownfish to tuck into?

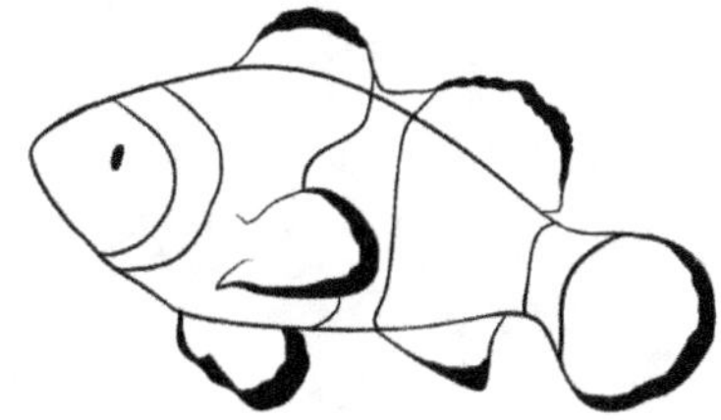

———

Clownfish are small, bright orange fish that live in warm, shallow ocean waters. They make their homes in sea anemones, which protect them with stinging tentacles while giving them a safe place to hide. In return, the clownfish keeps the anemone clean and helps chase away intruders. Can you imagine such a tiny fish living inside such a big, open world?

Seahorse

Seahorse

COLOR ME!

Seahorses come in many colors and patterns, from speckles to stripes. This outline is waiting for your creativity!

Can you trace over the seahorse and decorate it with bright colors, shapes, and designs to make it unique?

Seahorses drift gently through the water, wrapping their curly tails around seaweed to keep from floating away. They use their long snouts to slurp up tiny bits of food! Though small, they blend in beautifully with plants and coral around them. Can you draw a seahorse's colorful home?

Turtle

ON MY WAY

This turtle is swimming toward the beach, but its path is not easy. Fishermen and pieces of trash are in the way!

Can you help the turtle by drawing a safe path it can follow to reach the shore? Maybe it will find some fish on the way!

———

Sea turtles spend most of their lives gliding through the open ocean. With strong flippers, they travel thousands of miles and can stay underwater for long stretches of time. Can you draw a turtle swimming in the open ocean, grazing on some seagrass, or napping on the warm sand?

Manta Ray

Ray

FRIENDLY NEIGHBORHOOD

Manta rays aren't alone in their ocean home! Can you draw other sea animals (like fish, turtles, or dolphins) that might share the same waters as this gentle giant?

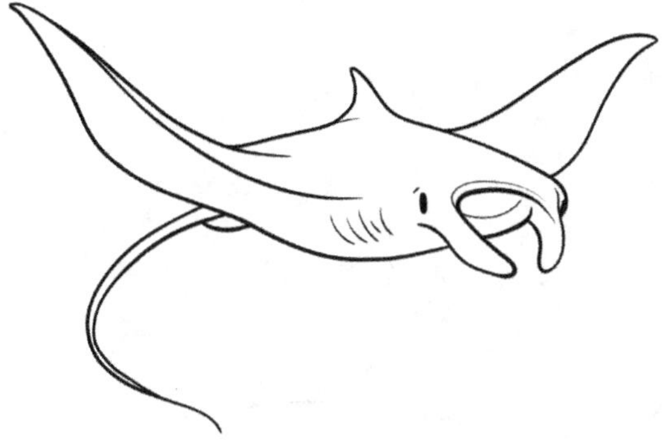

———

Manta rays glide through the ocean like gentle giants, moving their wide wings slowly as they swim through the vast ocean. They visit cleaning stations in coral reefs where little fish nibble away bits of dirt from their skin, keeping them healthy and bright. Can you draw a manta ray swimming in a reef or the open ocean?

Shark

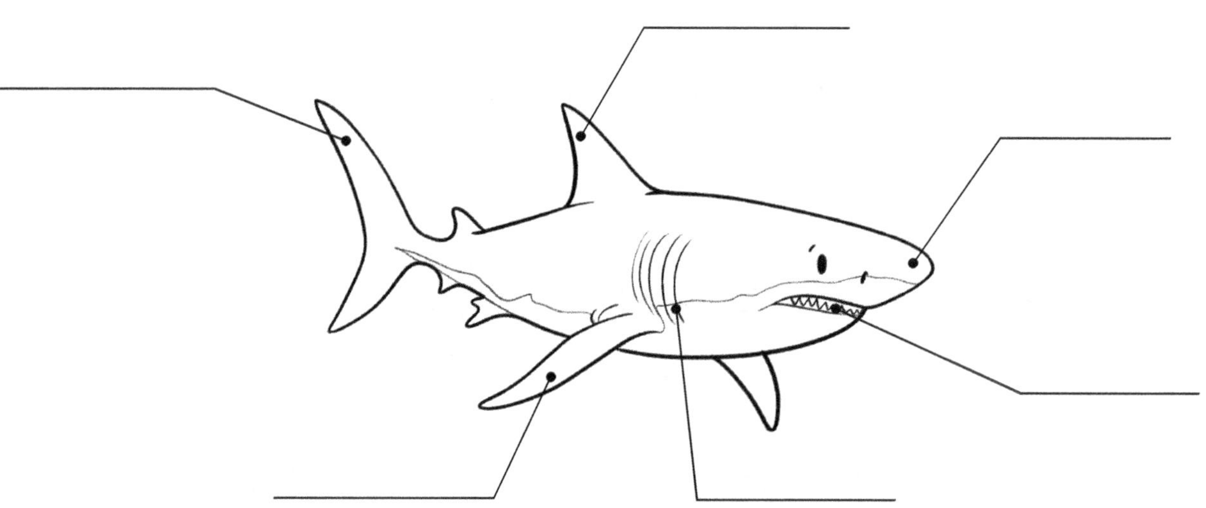

ANSWER KEY
Teeth
Gills
Dorsal Fin
Pectoral Fins
Tail Fin
Snout

MARINE BIOLOGIST

Sharks have special body parts that help them survive! Can you label the parts of this great white shark—like its fins, gills, tail, and teeth?

Great white sharks are powerful swimmers that roam the open ocean. They use their strong tails to move swiftly and their sharp senses to find food, even from far away. Though they look fierce, sharks play an important role in keeping the ocean healthy by balancing the food chain. Can you draw a vast ocean with other sea animals behind this shark?

Manatee

SEA BUFFET

Manatees love to snack all day long! They love sea grass, seaweed, and other plants.

Can you draw some colorful plants on the plate that a manatee might eat?

Manatees are gentle giants that drift slowly through warm, shallow waters. They spend their days munching on seagrass and floating near the surface to breathe. Sometimes called "sea cows," manatees move so peacefully that small fish often swim right beside them. Can you draw a manatee lazing around in the water?

Sea Lion

AQUATIC PLAYGROUND

This sea lion pup is exploring a tide pool, but not everything here belongs! Some items are natural and some are left by humans.

Can you circle the things that belong in the tide pool and cross out the things that don't?

Sea lions love to play along rocky shores, diving and splashing in cool ocean waves. Curious and quick, they peek into tide pools to look for crabs, starfish, and shells hidden among the rocks. When they're not exploring, sea lion pups rest close to their mothers, soaking up the sun. Can you draw a safe place for the sea lion pup to play?

Whale Shark

Shark

TO EAT OR NOT TO EAT

Whale sharks only eat tiny creatures they can filter from the water. Some of the items below belong in a whale shark's meal, and some do not!

Can you circle the things this gentle giant would eat and cross out the things it wouldn't?

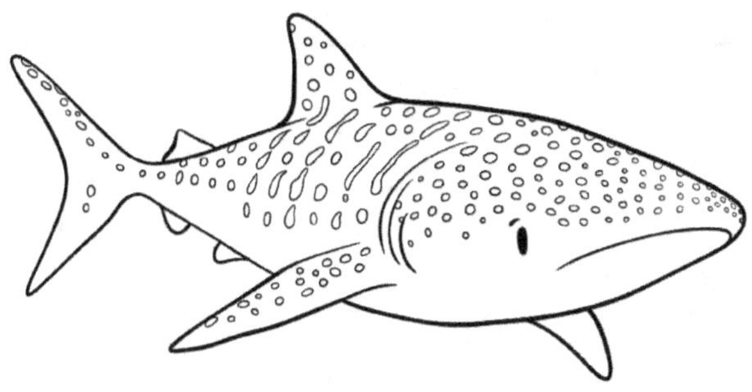

Whale sharks are the biggest fish in the ocean, but they're also gentle giants. They glide slowly near the surface, surrounded by smaller fish that follow in their wake. Can you draw this giant gliding in the ocean with some friends?

Pufferfish

SNEAK ATTACK!

This little crab has startled the pufferfish! When a pufferfish feels threatened, it puffs up really large to scare away potential threats.

Can you draw what you think a puffer fish would look like all puffed up?

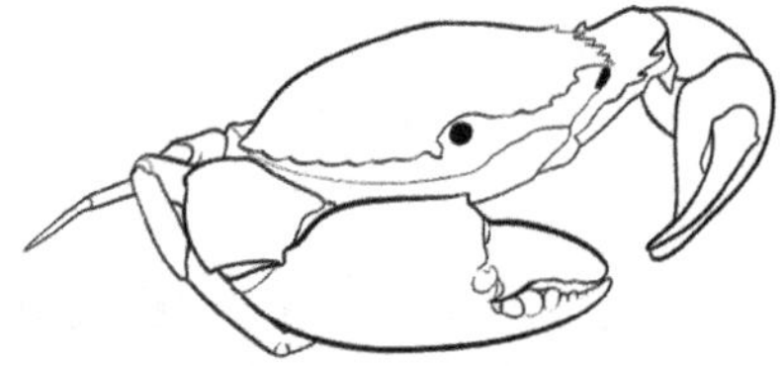

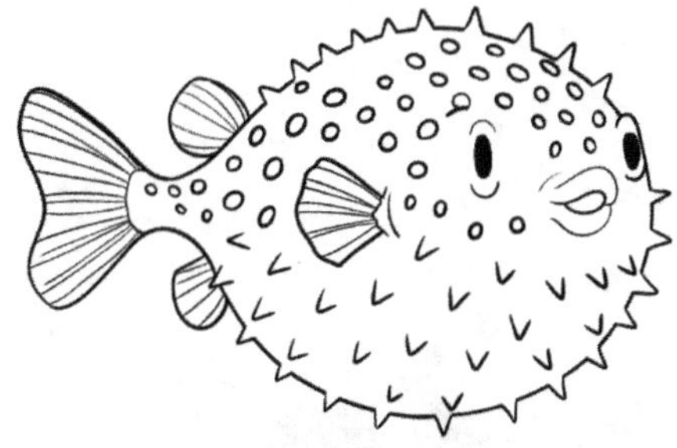

Puffer fish are small and curious creatures that live in warm ocean waters. They love coral reefs and being around other fish! Can you imagine the colorful, busy environment that a puffer fish would call home?

Orca

Orca

SOUND WAVES

Orcas use sound to "see" underwater—this is called echolocation! This orca sent out clicks and found a rock nearby.

Can you draw something else in the water for the orca to discover with its sound waves? Maybe a fish, a seal, or even an iceberg!

Orcas, also called killer whales, are powerful and intelligent hunters. They live in cold ocean waters near the Arctic and Antarctic, where icy waves crash against rocky coasts. Orcas travel together in family groups called pods, working as a team to catch fish, seals, and even squid. Can you draw this orca's icy home? Maybe with some family members nearby?

Marlin

SWEET TREAT

Marlins are skilled hunters, but they don't eat everything they see! Some of the items above are things a marlin would eat, and others are not. Can you circle what this marlin might catch for dinner and cross out what it wouldn't?

———

Marlins are some of the fastest fish in the sea! With their long, pointed bills and strong tails, they can leap high out of the water as they chase smaller fish near the surface. They live in the open ocean, where the water is deep and blue and full of movement. Can you draw a marlin gliding through the ocean?

This edition first published in North America in 2026 by Staggs Collection Press
ISBN 13: 979-8-9949754-2-8

Published by Staggs Collection Press